DATE DUE

Demco, Inc. 38-293

Russian AMERICANS

SPIRIT
of America®

Russian AMERICANS

By C. Ann Fitterer

The Child's World®
Chanhassen, Minnesota

Russian AMERICANS

Published in the United States of America by The Child's World®
PO Box 326 • Chanhassen, MN 55317-0326 • 800-599-READ • www.childsworld.com

Acknowledgments
The Child's World®: Mary Berendes, Publishing Director

Editorial Directions, Inc.: E. Russell Primm, Emily Dolbear, Sarah E. De Capua, and Lucia Raatma, Editors;
Linda S. Koutris, Photo Selector; Image Select International, Photo Research; Red Line Editorial and Pam
Rosenberg, Fact Research; Tim Griffin/IndexServ, Indexer; Donna Frassetto, Proofreader

Photos
Cover/frontispiece: A large family of Russian refugees upon their arrival in New York in 1921

Cover photographs ©: Library of Congress; David & Peter Turnley/Corbis

Interior photographs ©: AKG-images, Berlin, 6; Ann Ronan Picture Library, 7; AKG-Images, Berlin, 8 top;
Getty Images, 8 bottom; AKG-Images, Berlin, 9, 10 top, 10 bottom; Corbis, 11 top, 11 bottom; Getty
Images, 12; AKG-Images, Berlin, 13 top; Corbis, 13 bottom, 14, 15, 16; AKG-Images, Berlin, 17 top; Getty
Images, 17 bottom; Corbis, 18, 19; Topham/ImageWorks, 20; Getty Images/Photodisc, 22; TRIP/B. Turner,
23; Getty Images/Eyewire, FD001677; Getty Images, 25; Corbis, 26, 27 top, 27 bottom, 28 top, 28 bottom.

Library of Congress Cataloging-in-Publication Data
Fitterer, C. Ann.
  Russian Americans / by C. Ann Fitterer.
    p. cm.
Includes index.
Summary: A brief introduction to Russian Americans, their historical
backgrounds, customs and traditions, their impact on society, and life
in the United States today.
  ISBN 1-56766-158-0 (Library Bound : alk. paper)
  1. Russian Americans—Juvenile literature. 2. Immigrants—United
States—Juvenile literature. [1. Russian Americans.] I. Title.
  E184.R9 F58 2003
  305.891'71073—dc21
                    2001007387

14   17   24

Contents

Chapter ONE

Leaving Russia

THE PEOPLE OF AMERICA HAVE ROOTS IN countries all around the world. For hundreds of years, people from other countries left their homes to start a new life in America. Some groups have been in America for many years. Others have been in America for only a short time.

Once they landed at the port of New York, immigrants were inspected before being allowed to enter the country.

The people who have come to America from Russia are among the more recent groups of **immigrants**. Most of them arrived in the last 130 years. It is hard to identify the **typical** Russian immigrant because the word *Russian* is used to describe many different groups. These groups live across a very large part of Asia and their **cultures** are not all the same. Some groups of Russian people were even at war with one another in the past. As a result, no single culture or group in America stands out as being typically Russian. The one thing they have in common is that they speak the Russian language. Most of these people came to the United States to escape dreadful poverty and powerful leaders who gave them no freedom.

Alexander II, the Russian czar who freed the serfs in 1861

Since the 1500s, Russian people had lived under powerful leaders called czars. The czars made their own rules and punished those who did not follow them. They made slaves of most of the people. These slaves, called **serfs**, were owned by a few wealthy landowners. The serfs lived poorly and received little or

Interesting Fact

▶ Some Russian bagels are so hard that they must be dunked in tea to soften them.

no education. The czars of Russia did not try to make the country better or to improve the way people lived.

Some wealthy Russians were able to escape during the 1700s and 1800s. These people were educated and came from the middle class. They moved to America because the Russian government had too much control over their lives.

Families in Russia often lived in very poor conditions.

In 1861, all the Russian serfs were given their freedom. Many of them did not know what to do with it though. They had no money to buy land. They were not educated. They had no skills, so they could not get work.

A church in Moscow, the capital of Russia, in 1900

For hundreds of years, the Russian leaders had not made the people's way of life more modern. So, by 1900, although life in other countries was different from what it had been in the 1500s, life in Russia had not changed.

There had been no discoveries or new inventions. There was a lot of disease but very little medicine. Few people could read or write. Living conditions were terrible.

As a result, a large group of Russian people came to America between 1870 and 1920. These were poor people who were hoping for a better life. They wanted freedom from the government's control. Many of them wanted religious freedom, or the freedom to choose the religion they wanted.

The next large group of Russians arrived around 1920. A revolution in Russia in 1917 had put a new government in charge. Russia had become the Soviet Union. These Russian immigrants were different from the poor people who had come in the last 50 years. They were

V. I. Lenin, who led the Russian revolution in 1917

Villages in the Soviet Union were destroyed during World War II.

Mikhail Gorbachev, leader of the Soviet Union from 1985 to 1991

turning away from the new government in the Soviet Union. These people were wealthy upper-class Russians. At that time, the poor people stayed in the Soviet Union, thinking their lives would be better with the new government. Instead, their lives became much worse. Some described it as "living in a prison." Later, 35,000 Russians came to the United States as victims of World War II (1939–1945).

In the last half of the 20th century, America received two more groups of Russian immigrants. During the 1960s and 1970s, Russian Jews were allowed to leave the Soviet Union, and most of them came to the United States. Then, in 1991, the Soviet Union's form of government collapsed. The nation was once again known as Russia. Many other changes occurred. As a result, more than 1 million Russians came to the United States. Many of these immigrants were Russian Jews.

RUSSIAN PEOPLE LOVE weddings. In Russia most weddings last longer than one day. In America, too, Russian weddings follow many of the old customs.

A traditional Russian wedding in America may start with music in the morning at the bride's house. The bride's female relatives help her dress. The wedding couple joins the relatives at the church for the marriage ceremony. After the service, the guests return to the bride's house for a meal, usually breakfast. Later, the bride and groom receive bread from the guests. The bread is a symbol that the happy couple will never be hungry.

After breakfast, wedding pictures are taken at the house, and then everyone goes to the reception, which is usually held at a restaurant. The bride and groom meet the guests there as they arrive. Each guest drinks a toast, usually whiskey, to wish the bride and groom good luck.

After the evening meal and several hours of lovely Russian music, the bride, groom, and guests enjoy traditional dances and games. The party ends early the following morning and everyone goes home to sleep. The next afternoon, everyone comes back for another meal and a celebration that lasts into the night.

Chapter Two

Building a New Life

A market on New York City's Lower East Side, where many Russian immigrants chose to live

UNLIKE OTHER IMMIGRANT GROUPS, THE RUSSIAN newcomers did not create their own communities or take specific jobs or roles in the United States. In the 1700s and 1800s, they settled in the northern and eastern states. Many chose cities such as New York City; Philadelphia, Pennsylvania; Chicago, Illinois; Buffalo, New York; and Detroit, Michigan. These immigrants had few, if any, job skills. As a result, most took jobs in factories. The working conditions often were terrible and

they worked long hours— up to 12 or 14 hours every day. Most people made very little money in these jobs. Entire families lived together in just one or two rooms, and a five-room apartment may have been home to as many as 20 people. Clearly, life in America, for many Russian immigrants, was no better than life had been in Russia.

Russian immigrants often lived in crowded, noisy apartment buildings.

The Russian people had few freedoms in their home country. Most were not educated. They could not read or write English, and they did not know how to live in a place where people had freedoms. Often, they did not have enough experience to make good decisions. They were easily cheated in business deals. Dishonest Americans sometimes took advantage of them. The immigrants did not realize that U.S.

A group of Russian American marching for better working conditions

government officials would help them if they reported the dishonest people. The Russian immigrants had never lived in a country where the government was helpful and could be trusted.

Most of the wealthier, better-educated Russian immigrants who arrived in the United States around 1920 did not suffer as much hardship as the earlier immigrants. These new immigrants knew how to act around important people. They knew what to do at social events. Many got jobs in hotels and restaurants. Others

This cartoon from the 1890s shows Russian Jews moving into New York City, while other New Yorkers move out.

had hobbies such as sewing, horseback riding, music, and cooking during their lives in Russia. In America, they turned these hobbies into job opportunities. Some of the immigrants had been university professors. After learning English, they continued teaching in the United States.

This young Russian girl lived in a refugee camp in 1950.

The immigrants who arrived at the end of World War II received help from the U.S. government. Many had spent time in **refugee** camps in Europe before coming to the United States. In those camps, U.S. officials met with them and helped them find appropriate jobs in America. The immigrants were also given medical care. Then they were helped to their new home in America. And they quickly learned English.

Over the last 50 years, Russian immigrants have fit more easily into the American culture. A big **obstacle** to this, however, is learning English. Many Russians were doctors, lawyers, educators, and businesspeople in Russia, but they cannot work at those jobs when they arrive in America. First, they must learn to speak English. Often, they must take important tests that allow them to work in the jobs they had in Russia.

Life in America is quite different from life in Russia. This continues to be a difficult change for all Russian immigrants.

The different groups of Russian immigrants had unique experiences as they tried to settle in America. These differences kept them from preserving their Russian culture and **traditions** as much as they may have liked. Many also let go of their traditions in an attempt to become more American and not stand out as foreign.

A Russian-American food establishment in New York City

MANY RUSSIAN IMMIGRANTS, especially those who were serfs or came from poor families, had very little education when they were children in Russia. Many parents needed the children to work and to help earn money for the family. They were often **illiterate**, meaning they could not read or write. This did not change when they came to America. Many of their children also had little schooling. Instead, they worked in factories alongside their parents (above). As they got older, they did not have the skills needed for better jobs and had to continue doing unskilled work.

As those children grew up, however, they realized how important education is. America has good schools, and they made sure that their children attended. Russian-American children do very well in the American education system today. Many go on to college and hold important jobs.

Teaching the Russian culture is also important to Russian-American parents. One way to do this is by enrolling children in programs provided by the Russian Orthodox Church in **Exile**. These programs teach students about Russia's geography, dance, religion, music, language, and literature. Although these programs are not available everywhere in America, many Russian Americans benefit greatly from them in learning and preserving their Russian heritage.

Chapter THREE

Keeping Traditions Alive

Russian immigrants sailing in San Francisco Bay in 1923

BECAUSE RUSSIAN IMMIGRANTS ARE STILL coming into the United States, their experiences are different from those whose families have been here longer. Second- and third-generation Russian Americans have blended into American life. They tend to be well-educated, professional people. It is often difficult to realize they have Russian roots for the following reasons.

Earlier Russian immigrants were often separated

from other Russian people. This made it hard to keep traditions. They had few opportunities to speak their **native** language, except among family members. Many immigrants learned to speak English very quickly because they wanted to blend in with the rest of the American people. They did not want to be identified as immigrants.

A Russian Orthodox cathedral in San Francisco, California

Today, Russian communities in the United States are not as influenced by the Russian culture as they once were. As the children of the Russian immigrants grew up, they learned the American ways of life.

Often, these ways were quite different from the lifestyle their parents and grandparents had in the Russian-American community. As the children became young adults, they chose the American way of life and moved to different neighborhoods or cities. Some of these old-fashioned Russian communities, however, still exist today. Two very strong communities

A Russian-American couple dancing at a Hanukkah celebration at a Jewish community center

are in Brighton Beach, New York, and San Francisco, California.

Some Russian Americans have been able to keep their Russian traditions and culture alive through their places of worship. Many Russian immigrants came to America for religious freedom so their faith is important to them. They have strong ties to the people and traditions associated with their religion. It is estimated that Russian Jewish people make up half of the population of Russian Americans.

Russian Americans work in all types of jobs. Because the Russian school system often stressed math and science, many pursue jobs in those fields. Most Russian Americans continue their education beyond high school and work at professional jobs. As a result, Russian Americans, as a group, tend to have a higher income than other major ethnic groups in the United States.

Blending with the American culture has not been easy for Russian Americans. The clash of two different cultures has forced them to **adapt** quickly. As they achieve success in the United States, they do not forget their Russian heritage.

▸ Before there was hot running water in America, many Americans adopted a Russian bathing custom. The Russians put hot stones into a tub of water and sprinkled water on other hot stones to create steam. They then used small brooms to beat their skin, which made them feel even warmer.

The official name for Russia is the Russian Federation. The capital city of Russia is Moscow (below).

Russia is the largest country in the world and covers 6,592,850 square miles (17,075,400 square kilometers).

Because of its size, Russia has almost all types of landforms. It has lakes, it borders oceans and seas, and it has mountain ranges (opposite). The climate ranges from warm to very cold. Much of Russia is covered in snow for about six months of the year.

About 150,000,000 people live in Russia, mainly in the west, near Europe. The official language of the nation is Russian, but almost 100 languages are spoken in Russia.

Education is free through high school. Students must stay in school until they are 15 years old, but most complete the schooling. Many go on to colleges or universities.

Chapter FOUR

Influencing American Culture

OBVIOUSLY, RUSSIAN IMMIGRANTS HAVE NOT had as much time to influence American culture as groups who arrived hundreds of years ago. However, Russian culture has made significant contributions to American life.

For example, the Russian culture has had an impact on the foods we eat. One food that was introduced by Russians is sour cream. Today, sour cream can be bought in any grocery store. We use it in a variety of dishes.

Beef stroganoff is a tasty Russian dish that consists of beef in a sauce served over noodles or rice. Chicken Kiev is another delicious Russian dish. Both beef stroganoff and chicken Kiev are served in restaurants and in homes all across the United States.

Chicken Kiev is but one Russian dish that has become part of American culture.

Russian culture has had a great influence in the world of dance, too. Russian Americans, such as George Balanchine, have become famous in ballet. Balanchine was born in St. Petersburg and came to the United States in 1933. He helped found the School of American Ballet and was the artistic director for the New York City Ballet. His ballet companies brought many Russian ballet dancers to the United States.

Russian-American ballet dancer Mikhail Baryshnikov

Probably most famous among those dancers is Mikhail Baryshnikov. A brilliant and daring dancer, he is known for his highly developed technique. Baryshnikov left the Soviet Union in 1974 and joined the American Ballet Theater in New York City. Four years later, he joined the New York City Ballet. In 1990, he founded his own touring company called the White Oak Dance Project.

Writers in Russia felt controlled by their government for many years. They did not feel free to write as they wished, and many left

Writer Ayn Rand moved to the United States in 1926.

Russian artists are famous for creating religious icons that are found in churches all over the world.

Russia for that reason. Both Vladimir Nabokov and Alexander Solzhenitsyn lived in the United States for a time. Nabokov was best known for *Lolita*, published in France in 1938 and in the United States in 1959. He moved back to Europe in 1959. Solzhenitsyn was harshly criticized by the Russian government for his ideas. In 1974, Russia took away his citizenship and he moved to Switzerland. Two years later, he moved to the United States. Some of his novels include *Cancer Ward* and *The First Circle*. In 1990, Solzhenitsyn's citizenship in Russia was restored, and he moved back to that country in 1994.

An important Russian-American writer was Ayn Rand. Born in St. Petersburg in 1905, she moved to the United States in 1926 and became a U.S. citizen in 1931. Her best-known works are *The Fountainhead* and *Atlas Shrugged*.

Russian art has had a worldwide influence. Some of the most well-known pieces of Russian art are icons. These religious paintings are usually highly stylized portraits of Jesus, God, or the saints. They are painted according

Atmosphere and
Environment V,
*a work by sculptor
Louise Nevelson*

to rules made by the Eastern Orthodox
Church. Icons can be found in churches
throughout America.

Louise Nevelson was a sculptor who
was born in Kiev in 1900. She came to
the United States when she was five years
old and later studied at the Art Students
League in New York City.

Actress Alla Nazimova was born in Yalta
and performed at the Moscow Art Theatre
before moving to the United States in 1906.
She became famous on American stage and
screen, starring in plays such as *Hedda Gabler*
and *The Cherry Orchard* as well as the films
The Bridge of San Luis Rey and *In Our Time*.

*Pianist Irving Berlin is
remembered for writing
some of America's
favorite songs.*

In 1943, Russian-American Selman Waksman found a cure for **tuberculosis**, which until then had been the leading cause of death in the United States. He won the 1952 Nobel Prize for physiology or medicine.

Television is an important part of today's American culture. The first television was developed with technology created by Vladimir Zworykin. He came to the United States from Russia in 1919. An important Russian-American scientist is Jerome Isaac Friedman. He is a physicist who has done research about particles that form atoms. He shared the 1990 **Nobel Prize** for physics with two other scientists.

American music has also seen great contributions from Russian Americans. Igor Stravinsky, Aaron Copland, and Sergey Rachmaninoff were famous Russian-American composers whose music continues to be enjoyed throughout the world. Over the years, some of America's greatest conductors and performers have been Russian Americans.

Russian culture has always been rich in music, art, and literature. These traditions and others have contributed greatly to American culture.

Russian-American composer Aaron Copland

1500s Russian czars and wealthy landowners own serfs, who work as slaves.

1700–1800s Russian immigrants settle mainly in the northern and eastern United States.

1861 Serfs in Russia are granted their freedom.

1870 Large numbers of Russians begin arriving in America in search of a better life.

1905 Sculptor Louise Nevelson moves to the United States at the age of five.

1917 The Russian Revolution takes place. Russia becomes part of the Soviet Union.

1919 Vladimir Zworykin arrives in the United States from Russia.

1920 Another large immigration of Russians takes place. The immigrants are escaping life in the Soviet Union.

1926 Writer Ayn Rand moves to the United States and becomes a U.S. citizen five years later.

1939 World War II begins in Europe.

1940 Pianist Vladimir Horowitz moves to the United States and becomes a U.S. citizen four years later; Vladimir Nabokov arrives in America but returns to Europe in 1959.

1941 The United States enters World War II on December 7.

1945 World War II ends.

1960s–1970s Russian Jews leave the Soviet Union in large numbers. Most come to the United States.

1974 Ballet star Mikhail Baryshnikov leaves the Soviet Union and joins the American Ballet Theater.

1976 Writer Alexander Solzhenitsyn arrives in the United States but returns to Russia in 1994.

1991 The Soviet Union collapses. The largest portion of the former Soviet Union once again becomes known as Russia.

2002 Under the leadership of President Vladimir Putin, Russia joins forces with Western countries and becomes part of the North Atlantic Treaty Organization (NATO).

adapt (uh-DAPT)
To adapt is to change something to suit a new situation. Russian immigrants had to adapt quickly to the American culture.

cultures (KULL-churz)
Cultures are the ways of life, ideas, customs, and traditions of groups of people. The Russian culture varies among different groups of Russian people.

exile (EG-zile)
To be in exile is to be forced away from one's home. The Russian Orthodox Church in Exile provided programs for Russian Americans.

illiterate (ih-LIT-er-it)
A person who is illiterate cannot read or write. Some Russian immigrants were illiterate when they first arrived in America.

immigrants (IM-ih-grent)
An immigrant is someone who comes from one country to live permanently in another country. Russian Americans are recent immigrants to the United States.

native (NAY-tiv)
Something that is native belongs to a person because of where that person was born. Russians seldom spoke their native language in America.

Nobel Prize (noh-BEL PRIZE)
Nobel Prizes are international awards given each year for excellence in literature, economics, medicine, physics, chemistry, and for promoting peace. Selman Waksman won the Nobel Prize for medicine in 1952, and Jerome Isaac Friedman won the award for physics in 1990.

obstacle (OB-stuh-kuhl)
An obstacle is something that gets in your way or prevents you from doing something. Learning English was an obstacle for many Russian Americans.

refugee (ref-yuh-JEE)
A refugee is someone who is forced to leave his or her home because of war, persecution, or a natural disaster. Some Russian immigrants lived in refugee camps before coming to America.

serfs (SURFS)
Serfs are farm workers who are treated as slaves. Russian serfs were given their freedom in 1861.

traditions (truh-DISH-uhns)
Traditions are customs, ideas, and beliefs that are handed down for generations. Some Russians let go of their traditions when they moved to the United States.

tuberculosis (tu-bur-kyuh-LOH-siss)
Tuberculosis is a very contagious disease that usually affects the lungs. Selman Waksman found a cure for tuberculosis.

typical (TIP-ih-kuhl)
To be typical means that something or something has the traits that are usual or normal for a type or group. Describing a typical Russian immigrant is not easy.

For Further INFORMATION

Web Sites

Visit our homepage for lots of links about Russian Americans:
http://www.childsworld.com/links.html

Note to Parents, Teachers, and Librarians:
We routinely verify our Web links to make sure they're safe,
active sites—so encourage your readers to check them out!

Books

Greene, Meg. *The Russian-Americans.* San Diego: Lucent Books, 2002.

Lehrman, Robert. *The Store that Mama Built.* New York: Simon & Schuster, 1992.

Machlin, Mikki. *My Name Is Not Gussie.* New York: Houghton Mifflin, 1999.

Magocsi, Paul R. *The Russian Americans.* New York: Chelsea House Publishing, 1998.

Shiefman, Vicky. *Good-Bye to the Trees.* New York: Atheneum, 1993.

Places to Visit or Contact

American Carpatho-Russian Citizens Club
1006 Watson Boulevard
Endicott, NY 13760-2823
607-785-3100

Embassy of the Russian Federation
2650 Wisconsin Avenue, N.W.
Washington, DC 20007
202-298-5700

Russia House
1800 Connecticut Avenue, N.W.
Washington, DC 20036
202-986-6010

Index